Max's Box

Written by **KRISTEN AVERY** ■ Illustrated by **DENNIS NOLAN**

■ ScottForesman

A Division of HarperCollins*Publishers*

I can be Max the builder.

I can be Max the fisherman.

I can be Max the king.

4

I can be Max the cook.

I can be Max the painter.

I can be Max the astronaut.

I can be Max in a box!